The *Classic* HARLEY

The
Classic
HARLEY

MARK WILLIAMS

Photographs by
GARRY STUART

SMITHMARK

A Salamander Book

This edition published in 1993 by SMITHMARK Publishers Inc.,
16 East 32nd Street, New York, NY 10016

7 9 8 6

SMITHMARK books are available for bulk purchase for sales
promotion and premium use. For details write or call the manager
of special sales, SMITHMARK Publishers Inc., 16 East 32nd Street,
New York, NY 10016; (212) 532-6600

ISBN 0 8317 4292 5

All correspondence concerning the content of this
book should be addressed to
Salamander Books Ltd,
129–137 York Way, London N7 9LG, England

Credits

Editor: Richard Collins
Designer: John Heritage
Photographer: Garry Stuart
Filmset by Flair plan Photo-typesetting Ltd
Color reproduction P & W Graphics, Singapore
Printed in Italy

Additional captions

1 FXS Low Rider, with speedo and tacho set into old-time
Fat Bob tank.
2 Custom bike built by Rick Doss.
4 Softail custom FXSTC.
6 From dawn to dusk, the throbbing of V-twins fills the air.
8 Main Street, Daytona Beach.
10 Springer Softail, with gold plate, snakeskin, about $40,000
invested in it.

CONTENTS

INTRODUCTION

FOR HUNDREDS OF THOUSANDS of motor-cyclists the Harley–Davidson marque represents an expression of human spirit enjoyed by no other brand of vehicle, whether two- or four-wheeled, a name that's synonymous with a distinctive attitude and a proud lifestyle. Unlike the 'Big Four' Japanese companies that dominate the world market, the Harley–Davidson Motor Co. have been building motorcycles since 1903, but this depth of history is as important in human as it is in numerical terms, for the stamp of the Harley and Davidson families who founded the company has remained firmly embodied in its machines throughout this entire period.

This book is, in the diversity of its content, a testimony to the two families whose perceptive grip on the needs and tastes of American motorcyclists has been as constant as their desire to build and maintain a business that caters wholeheartedly to them. That Harley–Davidson motorcycles are now prized and demanded by increasing numbers of riders worldwide further emphasises the quality of their judgment . . . as well as that of their products.

But back in 1903 world markets were probably the last thing on the minds of Arthur and Walter Davidson and Bill Harley. Bill and Walter were working for Milwaukee's Barth Manufacturing Co. where a German immigrant colleague helped them perfect a crude, 3-horsepower, single cylinder engine based on the French DeDion design. The frame that they bolted this engine into was a unique, loop-frame unit considerably stronger than most of the diamond pattern designs that other fledgling manufacturers of 'powered bicycles' tended to utilise. Painted in gleaming black enamel with pin-striping and a logo design applied by the steady hand of Aunt Janet Davidson, this was one handsome and much admired machine. But despite temptations to follow their own star, the three men were sufficiently pragmatic to stay on the Barth payroll for a further three years, devoting only their spare time to the development of the Harley–Davidson Motor Co. and its motorcycles.

So by 1906 a mere fifty bikes had been produced and sold, at which point the founding trio were joined by the elder Davidson sibling, William A., and moved into a wooden shed built by the Davidsons' father in the family's backyard – a site now owned by the Miller Brewing Company. From this modest workshop the four men and their sole employee tripled their previous production total in just one year, and in 1908 some 450 bikes left the tiny 'factory', all of them developed from Bill Harley's original single cylinder, belt-driven design.

It wasn't until 1909 that the V-twin engine which is today synonymous with the company name appeared in its rudimentary 61cu. in. (1000cc) guise, the ever practical Bill Harley effecting this transformation by simply grafting an extra cylinder onto the existing single which, conveniently enough, was slanted forward to follow the line of the chassis downtube, resulting in the 45° angle that became its trademark. The bottom-end was beefed up to cope with the extra grunt of this first 'hog' and other modifications and additions followed thick and fast, including the first fully productionised motorcycle clutch (1912), the 'step-starter' and internal expanding rear brake (1914) and a 3-speed transmission (1915).

In the first two decades of the century mass production of the internal combustion engine and the industrial revolution of which it was a fundamental part opened up a huge new market for personal mobility. Then, as now, the motorcycle was in many ways the poor relation of the automobile, appealing more to blue rather than the white collar workers and in this transport-hungry marketplace there was a proliferation of ill-financed manufacturers producing badly designed and shoddily made machines. But by 1914 the Harley–Davidson Motor Co. had expanded rapidly to occupy nearly 300,000 sq. ft. and employ over one thousand five hundred people, such was the demand for its carefully conceived, high quality products.

Equally crucial to this success was Harley–Davidson's use of reliability as a vital marketing gambit and they entered their bikes in numerous endurance trials and lengthy road races, often ridden by the founders themselves. Their dominance in these events clearly bore fruit in sales which, by 1920, had reached over 28,000 a year but the Depression which followed in '21 saw that figure drop by almost two-thirds. Known as fair, even philanthropic employers, this meant difficult decisions for the founders, as it involved substantial lay-offs at the Juneau Avenue plant. But if times were tough for Harley, other manufacturers were completely wiped out by the 1920–21 recession, and this handed the Milwaukee company the lion's share of the low sales volumes that **were** achievable.

Mindful of the precarious effect the national economy could have on their company, Harley–Davidson cultivated sales to the military and police departments, developed their own line of sidecars (including those built solely for freight and deliveries) and a very popular 74cu. in. (1200cc) aero engine based on their fore-and-aft motorcycle engine. The 'twenties were also notable for the racing successes of the 21 cu. in (344cc) OHV 'peashooter' single in speedway and hill-climb events all over the world.

Late in that decade, the second generation of the two founding families was entering the company, continuing a tradition which even today is not lost on customers who eschew the faceless corporate identities of the Japanese multi-nationals. By the time of the 1929 Wall Street Crash there were six Davidsons and three Harleys working for the company, most of whom started out on the factory floor. They needed all their resolve and dedication to weather the Great Depression which followed, for while sales dropped only slightly in 1930 – from almost 21,000 units to some 17,600 – the 1931 model year saw this figure plummet to a paltry 10,000 units.

Fortunately the biggest casualties were the single cylinder machines, the newer V-twins proving especially attractive to bikers who could still afford motorcycles and, most particularly, America's police departments. Harley–Davidson also continued to sponsor their racing activities during the 'thirties, their biggest star being a quiet Canadian, Joe Petrali who, as well as being a versatile master of board-, dirt-track and hill-climb, provided valuable design input on Harley–Davidson's seminal OHV 'Knucklehead' engine (so called because of the shape of the valve housings), launched in 1936 and remaining in production for eleven years.

The Knucklehead, available in 61, 74 and 80cu. in. versions, featured a high-pressure lube system, 4-speed gearbox, roller-bearing cranks and greatly improved chassis and suspension, and the models they powered are still deemed by many to be the best looking ever. However, the star of the decade, certainly in financial terms, was the Servi-Car, a three-wheeler developed for the military at the behest of William S. Harley and Walter Davidson. This odd looking vehicle used the lowly 45cu. in. (737cc) side-valve motor mated to an enclosed, automobile-type differential via a 3-speed gearbox and chain drive. Versions of the Servi-Car were still being built well into the early 'sixties and during the WWII period alone nearly 89,000 units rolled off the production line.

Harley's fortunes fluctuated during the 'forties, aided by the slow demise of their only remaining domestic competitor, Indian, whose disastrous flirtation with lightweight 'British-style' motorcycles galvanised their commitment to the development of bigger and better V-twins. Harley's response to their threatening British invasion was initially confined mainly to their influence over American motorcycling racing's sanctioning body, the AMA, covertly governing such matters as capacity and compression ratios which favored Harley's old, side-valve 45cu. in. WR/WRTT machines against the technically advanced 500cc OHV British twins.

With the war over, a generation of homecoming servicemen found themselves unable to readjust to civilian life; many of them drifted around in the motorcycle gangs later glamorised by such films as **The Wild Angels** and **The Wild One**. These greasy jeaned, leather jacketed tearaways soon earned the 'outlaw' tag and their allegiance to what had become the quintessential American marque was a mixed blessing to Harley–Davidson, especially the more extreme gangs of Hell's Angels whose involvement in organised crime was later chronicled in Hunter S. Thompson's book of the same name. It's ironic that image of the outsider is the compelling motif that has led legions of well-heeled, middle-class motorcyclists into the arms of their nearest Harley–Davidson dealer.

But if outlaw gangs of variable notoriety harmed Harley's good name, the factory enjoyed continued growth through the late 'forties and 'fifties. 1948 saw the birth of the 'Panhead' motor, named after the flat-top castings protecting the new, hydraulically actuated tappets, an engine which for the first time featured mainly aluminum components and was inserted in the first Harley to use hydraulic front forks, unsurprisingly christened the Hydra Glide. Improvements to the Panhead's porting and exhaust design in 1950 were not so much to foster a performance image as to enable the motor adequately to propel the increasingly heavy touring-style bikes the company saw as its future, and it opened a new plant at Capital Drive, Wauwatosa, Wisconsin, in order to build them.

The Duo-Glide (with rear swingarm) and the Electra Glide proved the wisdom of their vision while the lackluster Model K 45 and 55cu. in. (900cc) were apparently intended as a sop to riders tempted by something in the European mould. But in 1957 that big and/or soft approach was brusquely sidelined when Harley launched the XL series, known colloquially then, and officially now, as the Sportster.

Initially produced in a 40bhp, 53.9cu. in. (883cc) form, the XL motor soon gathered power thanks to improved piston design, porting and valvegear and by 1962 the 55cu. in. engined Sportster was capable of running 13-second quarter mile drags with terminal speeds in the 115mph region. The Sportster kept on growing and wrought a number of variants including a mean looking 61cu. in. 'cafe-racer', the XLCR, which was the personal brainchild of Willie G. Davidson, grandson of William A., who remains head of styling at the time of writing. Today, 883 and 1200cc Sport-sters are Harley–Davidson's best-selling machines, even dominating capacity classes where they compete with the all-pervasive Japanese, who still strive unsuccessfully to emulate the feel and style of America's flying eagle.

The Sportster also spawned the alloy engined XR750, undoubtedly the most successful dirt- and flat-track racer ever, which was created by de-stroking the smallest, 883cc XL engine, fitting it with alloy barrels and dual Mikuni carbs. Good for 90bhp, the XR750 dominated American oval racing until the late 'eighties and inspired the XR1000 road-racer (nicknamed 'Lucifer's Hammer') which won Daytona's famous Battle of the Twins with factory dirt-track star Jay Springsteen at the helm in 1983.

Considering the popularity of oval track racing in America, and the mythology that lies behind it (going back to the board racing of the 'twenties), it may seem surprising that the factory never produced a road-going version of the XR750 to capitalise on its phenomenal success in the hands of latter-day heroes like Mert Lawwill, Cal Rayborn and the aforementioned Springsteen. The reason, of course, was cost; as ex-factory racing boss, the legendary Dick O'Brien explained to me, 'these engines were all hand-built, blue-printed and balanced, and without that they'd only make about half the power. Plus the cost of converting XRs to provide lighting and meeting emissions would've been prohibitive.'

Despite the impact of the Sportster, in 1959 the directors realised that they could no longer deal with the threat of lightweight European imports simply by trading on the emotive appeal of large V-twins. But rather than manufacturing bikes that required different production lines and offered smaller profits, the decision was taken to import a range of 125–250cc machines built by Aeronautica Macchi of Varese in Italy. William H. Davidson negotiated the purchase of 50% of the Aermacchi motorcycle division and head designer Wilbur Petri was despatched to Varese to 'American-ise' existing models and develop new ones for the US market. Unhappily the bikes, though well enough designed and built, were somewhat lagging behind the technical and performance standards then being offered by the British and, increasingly, the Japanese. And so despite a number of road-racing and motor-cross victories in the late 'sixties/early 'seventies, the Aermacchi experiment proved financially misplaced.

The 'sixties proved to be an era of turmoil for the company in other ways. In 1965 Harley–Davidson stock was offered to outside investors for the first time, which, by a circuitous and sometimes acrimonious route, led to the merger of the company with the American Machine & Foundry Corp in January 1969. Much needed development capital wasn't the only benefit of this union, for AMF had an empty bowling equipment and munitions plant in York, Pennsylvania, which was quickly adapted for motorcycle assembly, with Capitol Drive producing only engines and transmissions. Also during the 'sixties, the AMA's relaxing of restrictions on foreign marques hastened the defection of many factory riders to the Triumphs, BSAs and Nortons that were then dominating most areas of motorcycle competition where Harley had hitherto held sway.

At the end of the 'sixties, Harley–Davidson were selling only about 15,500 home-produced bikes per annum and the oil crisis of the early 'seventies (affecting haulage costs between the company's three plants perhaps more than it harmed actual sales), and the alleged 'dumping' of vast quantities of Japanese motorcycles added to Harley–Davidson's woes. On the upside was an increasing awareness of the product among a non-motorcycling public through films and TV series like **Electra Glide in Blue** and **Then Came Bronson** and, in 1978, the US Treasury Dept's findings in favor of Harley–Davidson's protestations of dumping against three of the Japanese 'Big Four'. Their elation was offset just three month's later by the International Trade Commission's ruling that their activities had not harmed sales of Harley's very different model range.

Relationships between AMF and the 'old' Harley managers were strained by all this and more, and after protracted negotiations, twelve of the senior managers, led by Vaughn Beals and Willie G. Davidson, bought back their company from AMF for $75 million in 1981. A year later, revitalised by the introduction of the Evolution engine, which offered all the character of the redoubtable V-twins but none of the weaknesses and oil leaks, they sold off the Aermacchi plant to the Italian Castiglioni brothers (who founded their Cagiva/Ducati empire there) and began a bold new era.

The older, increasingly ill-finished models that had somehow seen them through the 'seventies were running out of steam and the 'Evo' engine, developed with the aid of AMF money, was gradually introduced in the different capacities demanded by the range. But chassis and transmissions also had to keep pace and belt-drive, mono-shock 'Soft-tail' rear-ends and even a modern version of the 'Springer' front forks enabled Harley–Davidson to marry modern technology with their customers' insistence on the folksy looks and character of its all-American heritage.

The company's ability to carry off this has been fueled by a combination of tenacious vision and traditional values, on the one hand maintaining the image and nature of the abundantly torquey, slow-revving V-twin but within new technological and legislative parameters, on the other, expanding the marketplace to embrace a new generation of owners with clever marketing, a broad range of factory-customising options, clothing and merchandise, and their dedicated backing of the international Harley–Davidson Owners Group (HOG). Thus, in the 1990s with sales in excess of 100,000 units per annum, Harley–Davidson riders enjoy the camaraderie of a worldwide motorcycling brotherhood, secure in the knowledge that theirs is a unique motorcycle, usually in both senses of the word.

Mark Williams

20TH-CENTURY COWBOYS

THE URGE TO HIT THE ROAD comes as second nature to most motorcyclists, but to the Harley–Davidson rider that urge acts as a lifeforce. True, Harleys aren't the fastest, sharpest handling machines, but whether ridden in anger or in the sure-footed, laid-back style that best suits them, they're the most satisfying bikes on any road.

As the twentieth century began to take shape, for many Americans Harleys replaced the horse as a means of independent transport, literally as well as a metaphorically. Ever a restless, mobile nation, America embraced the internal combustion engine with the same zeal and affection that helped it shape its destiny astride a horse in the previous century. And like the iconoclastic loners who tamed the West, a particular breed of men took to the iron horse – as exemplified by Milwaukee's finest.

In those early days, it wasn't just Harley–D's superior reliability that endeared them to the serious, if budget-conscious rider, nor was it the affable, lazy torque of the big, 45° V-twin, for there was something about Harleys that reflected the spirit of the times. The bikes, like their riders, were straightforward, no-frills animals that delivered the goods and, while distinctive in their own right, responded empathetically to their owners' input. Harley–Davidsons were the motorcycles of choice for Americans confident of who they were and where they were headed; that still holds good today. Now, as in past decades, a Harley is known and admired for what it is, where it comes from (and how easy it is to fix!). If you're riding a Harley, you're making a statement about America and who you are, which makes a firm foundation for wherever else you happen to be headed. It's a good feeling, and with it comes a mutual respect that works three ways – between rider, machine and the world at large. Nowadays that equation has infiltrated other cultures, for in a world of frantic and often needless change, a Harley–Davidson says something about its owner that no other motorcycle can. That's why people ride 'em.

Figures in a landscape somehow have
more presence when they're
chugging steadily along on Harleys,
for its takes a special kind of bond
between man and machine to make
that presence felt against the looming
majesty of America's Big Country.
Harley riders have that confidence.

Nowadays the Electra Glide range encompasses a range of styles from the relatively pared down 'Sport' to the full-house 'Ultra Classic Tour Glide', all of them powered by Harley's biggest V-twin, the 80cu. in. (1340cc), rubber-mounted version of the Evolution engine. What they also have in common is a fuel capacity of four US lead free gallons. The fuel requirements of their riders are something few of them will share.

Harley–Davidson's top-of-the-range Electra Glide is the traditional choice for the discriminating, long-distance motorcyclist and in its 'Ultra Classic' guise it offers just about everything required for relaxed two-wheeled touring. Except, that is, for food and drink. But then an essential ingredient in the Big Tour is the pleasure of stopping off at some unhurried, down-home truck stop or diner to re-fuel the body, as well as the bike.

Not everyone's idea of life on the open road involves kitting himself up with on-board hi-fi and cruise control astride a fully-faired dresser. Harley–Davidson offers plenty of choice when it comes to suiting any rider's needs and here a pair of lightly customised FXR-series models propel a serious looking trio beneath a big blue sky. The style is quintessentially free-wheeling, 20th-Century Cowboy; wind-knotted manes and bugs in the teeth are part of the deal, but then so is the exhilaration of being wedded to the scenery as the world roars by.

One of the many aspects of a real hog that's confounded oriental attempts to emulate the soul of a Harley–Davidson lies in its riding style. And one good reason why it's so elusive is because every Harley owner adapts his riding posture to suit himself and the sort of journeys he makes. However, the laid-back, low-down seating, allied to a pair of high'n'wide handlebars, favors the sort of road burning many riders specifically buy their Harleys for. Forward mounted foot-pegs and attendant control levers complete an easy riding position which in turn augured an image that was catapaulted into the public consciousness thanks to Dennis Hopper's seminal 1969 movie, **Easy Rider**.

Today's easy riders may not be looking for the soul of America through a haze of illegal substances, but whether in packs, in pairs or running solo, it's easy enough to experience the pervasive grip of the nation's heritage from the saddle of a Milwaukee V-twin. Of course, only a relatively small number of Harley–Davidson owners are **bona fide** free-wheelers who can take off wherever and whenever they want, but there are days in every Harley owner's life when he can get out there and relax into the mind-set of the roadgoing adventurer.

Something about the bikes and the stories they've had to tell insinuates its way under the skin of anyone who values the freedom that travel can bring, but it goes deeper than that. On the one hand, in the pressured, increasingly regimented world that most of us inhabit, a quick blast down the highway is enough to clear the mind of excess baggage and untap a little adrenalin. On the other, a week or two's vacation provides the opportunity for many desk-bound Harley owners to revitalise the spirit and remind themselves where they're **really** headed. Maybe some, like the Texan biker on the right, haven't seen a desk job in years.

A lot of folk are surprised when you tell them you're taking a journey of several hundred, or even several thousand miles on a motorcycle, but they're usually people who've never ridden a Harley. But after a short baptism on the pillion seat, they may well understand why you're doing it . . . they may even demand to come along! But riding solo is the way to go for most riders with serious miles to kill. Out there on your own, you take the road and the day at your own pace, getting as close to your bike as any human being has a right to do, serenaded and soothed by the steady throb of the V-twin.

Come twilight, most riders are ready for a change of pace and then even the hard-riding loner is usually ready for a few cold beers and a little company. Find yourself a bar where there's a hog parked outside, and you're likely to meet kindred spirits to swop road-talk with; independent though he may be, a Harley rider is never truly alone.

And like their forebears from an earlier era, when the trip's finally over, Harley riders kick back and relax, or celebrate, in whatever way suits them. Maybe the roving horsemen of the Old West couldn't catnap in the saddle with quite the same ease as a twentieth-century cowboys can aboard their iron horses . . .

. . . but that apart, their lifestyles do share certain similarities, such as a tendency toward hirsute (if rather well groomed) ruggedness, and an appreciation of ladies who in turn appreciate their very particular angle on life. Without Harley–Davidson, life would be the poorer for them, and indeed for America.

ANGELS AND OUTLAWS

THE DIFFERENCES BETWEEN A COWBOY and an outlaw were often vague a century ago and in some respects remain so today. Whereas the slogan 'Live to Ride–Ride To Live' might be acceptable to the guy whose main inspiration stems from his motorcycle, to those on the wilder fringes of that same world it has a more menacing ring. Hell's Angels, Satan's Slaves, Road Rats . . . whatever their tag, motorcycle outlaws elect to reject laws that most other bikers grudgingly accept. And sometimes they actively perpetrate crimes that not even the most amoral biker can condone, stuff like drug-running and contract violence. Condemn this though we must, those who ride American steel and have tasted the freedom that it proffers often harbor a sneaking admiration for those who've taken that irrevocable step over the civilised threshold. The outlaws first came to prominence after WWII when many returning servicemen found themselves unable to adjust to a civilian life that condemned overt machismo and required respect for human niceties that had been bombed out of them. Without jobs or direction and with motorcycles as the only constant in their lives, these disaffected individuals gravitated toward each other and into a lifestyle with its own codes of honor. But honor doesn't pay the bills, so these fledgling brigands took to crime to support the partying that quickly became foremost among their avowed goals. Territorial considerations soon spawned internecine confrontations which, in a freely gun-toting society, meant that blood soon started spilling.

At a time when America was too busy growing up and getting rich to notice the scabrous activities of a small, obstinate minority, the outlaw gangs grew in number and so did their criminal activities. But if those who suffered and those who dwelt in ignorance allowed the outlaws to enjoy a kind of illicit normalcy, other, more influential forces found them rather fascinating: movie makers, and journalists of varying legitimacy viewed bike gangs with prurient interest, and so did the rest of us.

The seductive appeal of the outlaws
initially lies with their look. The
'patches' emblazoned on leather and
denim, chains and studs adorning
boots and belts, the tattoos
decorating their flesh – all images
that have been gradually co-opted
by motorcycling's mainstream.

Nowadays virtually every motorcycle club in the world has its own logo stitched into a patch or set into an enamel badge, and the heavy, hard-wearing leather and footwear initially associated with the motorcycle gangs enjoys the dual merits of offering both macho fashion credibility and sensible protection which few bikers can ignore. But outlaws don't really care about what the rest of us make of **their** uniforms; they wear them to identify themselves and stand apart from other gangs and, of course, the straight world they've rejected.

But although these images are touched with an insolence and *frisson* of the forbidden, it wasn't so much the visual as the anti-social that attracted the media to the outlaws. The idea of real-life outsiders, the 'one-percenters' as they called themselves, was utterly compelling to those looking to pounce on any social deviation and blow it up into controversy. On holiday weekends in the early 'fifties, bike gangs began descending on hick Southern Californian towns to party and brawl, the upshot of which was local outrage and, in 1953, the seminal Laslo Benedek/ Stanley Kramer film, *The Wild One*.

Marlon Brando's laconic nihilism in *The Wild One* and the random violence that erupted around him set the tone for a whole genre of bike gang movies, most of which were made a decade later. More immediate were the PR effects of the film; suddenly it was cool to be an Angel or a Slave and membership grew rapidly, as did a proliferation of new chapters and yet more luridly named gangs. But joining the outsiders involved induction ceremonies that were – and often still are – decidedly stomach-turning. Apocryphal though they may perhaps be, tales of biting off chickens' heads, drinking menstrual blood and riding head on toward a gang member to measure resistance to chickening-out were rites of passage that have long been the stuff of outlaw legend, which at least ensured that only serious bad asses applied for membership.

During the 'sixties the outlaw sub-culture gained momentum and notoriety via such films as Roger Corman's **The Wild Angels** and Lee Madden's **Hell's Angels '69**, the latter actually featuring Terry the Tramp, Sonny Barger and other **bona fide** members of the infamous Oakland Hell's Angels. The same gang provided source material for Hunter S. Thompson's definitive volume, **Hell's Angels: A Strange and Terrible Saga of the Outlaw Motor Cycle Gangs**, whose graphic accounts of brutality and illegality were far removed from the knockabout antics portrayed by Hollywood.

Thompson's book got him into some trouble with his subjects, but this was as nothing compared to **Rolling Stone** magazine's lengthy exposé of the Angels' drug manufacturing and trafficking activities which led to big jail sentences for some of their leaders. But if outlaw involvement in organised crime peaked around the turn of the decade, their influences continued to spread far and wide.

Not only were second generation gangs maintaining their territories and influences but black and hispanic bike gangs were starting to get in on the act. Arguably, these ethnic based motorcycle outlaws were formed more for reasons of camaraderie or solidarity against the machinations of the white gangs than they were for reasons of profitable villainy.

The outlaw influence inevitably found its way overseas, gathering converts as the Japanese exports all but crippled the UK motorcycle industry and European bikers turned to Harleys as a symbol of their own ethnicity. So just as riding a Harley–Davidson in Europe bespoke a certain attitude, joining a bike gang bestowed the additional benefit of strength in numbers.

Which is not to say that the outlaw gangs of France, Germany, Holland and Britain were entirely ill-disposed to a bit of muscle-flexing, but their involvement in crime was usually limited to a bit of small scale drug-dealing and bike-theft. However, as an outlaw friend once told me, 'We never steal bikes from other Angels, and we don't ever steal Harleys . . . 'cause that ain't right.' And woe betide any common bike thief who makes the mistake of stealing an Angel's Harley, for that's just about the ultimate outlaw sin.

Nowadays there's often a public relations officer within the tightly controlled outlaw hierarchies, for the gangs are more anxious to present a positive image to the world, if only to distract unwelcome attention from the authorities. Outlaw gangs also help raise money for all manner of charities and, particularly in Europe, organise motorcycle events that are open to all. Even politics are not beyond the influence of gangs such as the Vietnam Vets motorcycle clubs who put pressure on, as well as rebel against, an establishment that easily forgets the sacrifices made by those who fought a later war.

The slogans offered by the Vietnam Vets are not so much 'Off The Pigs', but rather 'Release Our POWs', and the Harley–Davidsons they ride are decorated not so much with winged eagles and scenes of sword and sorcery, but death heads wearing tin helmets and battle fatigues. It's also true to say that, in many respects, rivalries between the different chapters and factions within the outlaw netherworld have largely disappeared, the 'strength in numbers' philosophy having permeated the American scene in much the same way it did in Europe.

Most of the original outlaw gangs that still flourish in the 'nineties support the Vietnam Vets because they understand from their own ancestry where these guys are coming from. Indeed, there's a certain pride in the support, tacit and otherwise, that they offer the Vets and this mutual admiration is very much in the original spirit of 'outsiders looking after their own'. Which is exactly as it should be.

When bike gangs get together these days it's rarely to exercise bloody vendettas or drift into some other, less formal fist fights; more likely to party, or even demonstrate behind a cause, such as the much reviled anti-helmet legislation, or the MIAs – American servicemen still believed to be held in Vietnam, though officially designated as 'Missing In Action'. So when they do come together you'll witness not just the stirring sight of flowing hair and throbbing metal.

. . . but also notice some quirky, personal protests such as the MIA supporter (left) who carries his bamboo cage around from rally to rally, and then incarcerates himself in it to symbolise the plight of his Vietnam Vet brethren. You might feel that the new breed of politicised outlaw gangs are a little naïve in the causes they espouse, but maybe that's not an argument you would want to pick with them!

One aspect of the outlaw philosophy
that remains unquestionable (and
unquestioned) is their staunch
nationalism. They may flaunt many
of the country's social conventions,
and the laws of the land may often
incur their abject disdain and denial,
particularly those that come under
the heading of 'Traffic Legislation',
but America is their country and
they're damn well proud of it. Sure,
an outlaw's vision of God's Own
Country is probably a little different
from that of the average Joe, but
when all is said and done, they
share allegiance to the same flag.

Much of this has to do with the bike gangs' partisan attitude toward the Harley–Davidson and their consequent hatred of oriental ironware, generating bellicose T-shirt slogans which are invariably underpinned with a strip or flash of the Red, White and Blue. What would happen if, as was once on the cards, the Milwaukee company had sold out to the Japanese, one shudders to think!

And so the Stars and Stripes feature heavily in the iconography of the outlaw gangs: going right back to Peter Fonda (aka 'Captain America') and his Panhead chopper in **Easy Rider**, gas tanks decorated with the flag motif have long been popular with customisers. Less convoluted patriotic images in the shape of Stars and Stripes patches, bandanas and T-shirts can been seen in any outlaw's wardrobe.

49

Anti-Japanese sentiment finds expression in the T-shirt worn by the guy on the Glide, the slogan on which refers to the practise of torching worn-out oriental roadsters at many a biker rally, and not just those organised by outlaw gangs. Along with these 'Bike Roasts', many of these events also feature 'Jap Smashing' contests where willing if perhaps inebriated participants try and break up a hapless Honda or Kawasaki with a fencing hammer in the shortest possible time.

A rather less violent expression of this fierce loyalty to the home-grown marque can be seen at a Florida bar much patronised during Daytona's Bike Week, namely the 'Japanese Hanging Garden'. This well-loved landmark features numerous long-expired Japanese motorcycles forlornly suspended from a tree, their progressive states of decay being recorded with all due ridicule by the regulars who visit it annually, all of them Harley-mounted, naturally!

How seriously one should take the American outlaws' xenophobia and their espousal of certain causes is a matter for debate, although probably not very serious debate, but one thing is for sure and that's the wry sense of humor that accompanies it. Whether it's a biker wearing a pastiche of the traditional outlaw 'colors' which features both a tin-helmeted skull and a wreath of marijuana leaves **under** the Panama red banner – while making sure that there's a Harley–Davidson logo at the bottom to keep it all vaguely in context

. . . or the seriously bearded, barrel-chested and presumably Texan biker whose skull head design adorning his Harley's gas tank is in mild contrast to the tattoos decorating vast tracts of his own body, including a Confederate flag flowing down one side of his back and a well-needled forehead!

Rebellious rhetoric laced with a rough-knuckled and often lewd humor also find their way into the buttons and badges and baseball hats of the disaffected men and women who live in, or in the shadow of the motorcycle outlaw's world: always were, always will be. And I guess that consistency is just one small sign that the phenomenon of the outlaw gangs is as enduring and durable as, well, as the Harley–Davidson motorcycle.

KINGS OF CUSTOM

THE CURRENT SUCCESS of the Harley–Davidson Motor Co. is due in no small part to the fact that it offers its customers an infinite number of variations on a basic theme. These days very few bikes leave the showrooms in stock specification, for the factory offers an almost bewildering array of color schemes and authorised bolt-on extras via the dealer network, which means extra bucks for Harley–Davidson and a degree of exclusivity for the owner, only a relatively recent development in the company's history. Up until the mid-'eighties, adapting your hog to your own tastes was a job you either undertook yourself, or consigned to any one of the thousands of specialists that maintained the individuality of the Harley–Davidson around the world. This meant that not only were Harley owners inclined to personalise a machine that otherwise resembled a zillion others, but that the ongoing consistancy of design and engineering made it economical for aftermarket manufacturers to offer performance and cosmetic add-ons.

This potential for customising one's machine reached its zenith in the late 'sixties and 'seventies when the vogue for 'choppers' exploded across the world from its fertile, if sometimes bizarre roots in Southern California. A chopper is – literally – a chopped down motorcycle stripped of all items considered inessential to its performance; yet most of the bikes subjected to such treatment were quickly appended with all manner of gee-gaws that rendered them heavier and less wieldy than they were before. Not that their owners cared, for those who altered their Harleys, did so primarily to make a statement about themselves. This much is obvious whenever Harley–Davidsons are to be found **en masse** today, for what looks an immaculate XR750 racer but is in fact a craftily disguised Sportster may be nudging alongside a rather less pristine Knucklehead chopper with five foot long springer forks, all evidence of the individuality that is Harley–Davidson.

High'n'wide handlebars, extended springer forks and chrome-on-everything epitomise the chopper image. Early examples of the genre, such as these two Knuckleheads, often lacked front brakes which, together with radically altered steering geometry, made for cautious riding.

The fact that American roads are longer and straighter and their corners less acute than those of most other nation's means that the slow steering, under braked, rigid framed choppers can in fact make their way without too much drama provided, of course, that their pilots know the deal. This may be why some of the more extreme, and certainly the better constructed, custom Harleys belong in more mature hands. Many of these older bikers actually go touring on their machines, packing what little they need for a gentle chug through a warm Southern climate into a pair of leather saddlebags.

One of the favored routes taken by early customisers was to exaggerate by extension, sometimes resulting in choppers that were fifteen feet long from the far edge of their skinny front tyres back to the sky-grasping tip of their chromed 'sissy bars'. Exhaust pipes also underwent the same treatment, sometimes capped with pseudo fish-tails which, while they added little extra power, did cut a certain dash. Unrestricted air-filters remain a common modification which, unlike some of the custom exhaust systems, provide an increase in performance, as well as noise.

What may superficially be the easiest way of personalising your hog can just as easily turn out to be the most taxing, for the notion of simply changing a Harley's livery is to venture down a road that literally has no end. Custom paintwork is truly an art form and one that lends itself to the realisation of all manner of fantasy, although certain themes are well established within the airbrush artist's canon, one of which is the streaking flame.

On these pages you see three different variations of the stylised flame motif, superficially similar but actually very distinct both in their relative complexity and the subtlety of coloring. Each doubtless inspired by the bikes' owners, and spanning three decades of the Harley model range, these renderings involved many hours of preparation, masking the patterns, delicate layering of each color, finished off by several coats of clear lacquer to provide that vital depth of finish.

Even more unique custom-painted images demand even more painstaking execution, and a fine example of this can be seen on the left. Here a meticulously engineered, Evo-powered Harley is topped off with a beautiful, emerald metalflake gas tank bearing a meticulous facsimile of a gold Amex card, which features details of the actual machine. Whoever was responsible for it might well have a lucrative career ahead of them in forgery!

Although changing the visual identity of your beloved Harley is rarely undertaken lightly, roving custom-painters attend many of the larger motorcycle rallies to realise the whims of those that are ready to take the plunge. Demand for images of well-endowed, scantily clad adventuresses keeps many such artists in work all year round, though quality varies according to price. The lady in blue (top, right) is in the higher quality bracket, while the livery on the old, side-valve sidecar outfit (bottom, right) goes for humor rather than erotic fantasy.

Different eras provide inspiration for wildly different – and downright wild – examples of custom craft. The Panhead (top, left) features a 'fifties look with its rigid frame and authentic gas tank, but utilises a rear disc-brake and modern exhaust. In 1988, Harley's re-invention of the Springer front-end, coupled with its Softail chassis (in which a 'rigid' rear end is actually a clever mono-shock suspension), opened up a whole new Pandora's box of custom ideas – some of them less than subtly executed (below, left).

The company's lucrative re-cycling of its heritage isn't limited to the technical trickery embodied in the Springer and Softail, and includes anniversary specials such as the Sturgis 50th (above, right), which in turn prompted Messrs Custom Chrome to personalise what was already a limited edition which, ironically, substitutes paint for much of the brightwork! The Shovelhead (above, left) is less coy about showing a shine, although in other respects remains remarkably stock.

On the left is a cunning amalgam of Panhead top-end on Sportster engine cases. The modern, telescopic front end is off-set by a period-badged gas tank which features a neatly moulded-in tachometer and filler cap. The foot-boards, deeply valenced front fender and spoked wheels continue the retro theme, while the disc brake and trafficator lamps suggest more contemporary and pressing considerations . . . like safety.

Another, if not so subtle retro custom (above, right) incorporates highly stylised 'fifties design imagery with hi-tech paintwork and neon coloring. More discreet is the Panhead-look-alike, disc-braked cruiser (below, right) which employs a modern, Springer front-end mated to a rigid chassis replete with foot-boards. The fish-tail mufflers and front disc are actually contemporary factory options; the abundant but not excessively flashy chromework is not and is nicely complimented by the multi-toned grey paintwork. Check also the matching studded seat panels and leather tank strap.

Even by normal custom standards this Evo-engined special (above) reflects a fastidious attention to detail. Note how the base cherry-red paint used on the tank and fender is also employed – presumably in a heat-resistant finish – between the engine finning. Other neat touches include a row of warning lights set into the tank fascia, and extensive (and expensive) chroming of alloy engine cases, matched by highly polished, steel-braided oil lines.

Aftermarket carburettors are a tried and tested route to increase horsepower and torque, but adapting them to fit a Harley engine takes a little ingenuity. The twin-barrel example fitted to the elderly but beautifully prepared Shovelhead (above) sits neatly between the cylinders and is complimented by a oil pressure gauge tapped into the rear cylinder head. The paint job is pretty nifty, too.

The forward facing location of the carburettor fitted to this radically liveried, Evo-engined Springer Softail (above) may be intended to produce a ram-air effect, but the unequal length inlet tracts must make tuning a rather delicate affair.

This detail from yet another Springer Softail (right) reflects a somewhat less outrageous approach to the customers' craft, but nonetheless goes a little overboard in the chromework and engraving departments.

IMAGES OF DAYTONA

SINCE 1941 THE FIRST WEEK IN MARCH has marked the beginning of the motorcycling year for many Americans, because that's when the mounted hordes descend on the small Florida resort of Daytona Beach. Daytona is essentially about the annual bike races which originally took place on the vast strip of sand but which have been run at the Daytona Speedway track since the 'sixties. However, only relatively few of the motorcyclists who visit Daytona each year go to watch the racing, even when a Harley–Davidson factory team are making the running, as in 1983 when XR 1000-mounted Jay Springsteen won the Battle of the Twins at a top speed of 167mph.

No, the attraction of Daytona is to escape the cruel winters of the eastern seaboard and meet up with like-minded bikers, particularly like-minded Harley owners. Strictly a celebration of the biker ethos, this gathering of several thousand committed riders soon turns into a week long party where it's never hard to find some action.

That's mainly because there's very little to Daytona Beach but the beach itself, and a strip of shops, bars and restaurants that run parallel to the rear of hotels. 'The strip' is where most of the action takes place and in the 'seventies and early 'eighties all manner and varying degrees of wild behavior were to be found in the beers halls down Main Street.

Nowadays it doesn't get quite so crazy, not least because the local burghers and the police force have gotten tougher on drug abuse, drunken driving – or rather riding – especially when the two are combined. The American Motorcycle Association, who nominally sponsor Raceweek, are also mindful of the damaging effects that unwholesome images of bikers can have on the public at large and politicians in particular, which is why more and more fringe events during Raceweek are geared toward promoting motorcyclists as caring, socially aware citizens, just like you and me.

For all the ever increasing 'officially sanctioned' activity during Race-week, the enduring images of Daytona are those of impromptu events taking place routinely each day. A gaggle of Milwaukee hogs on the strip at dusk perfectly illustrates Daytona's 'tingle-factor'.

As befits its civic title, that long, wide strip of golden sand was originally Daytona Beach's major attraction, and during Bike Week it resumes much of its focal importance as bikers and their female companions cruise the beach to show off their iron and vast expanses of nubile tan.

There's a fifteen mile an hour speed limit on the beach – a far cry from the days when the factory Harleys sped up and down on their side-valve flat-trackers at over 100mph. Most of today's visitors don't mind the slow progress . . . it gives 'em more time to take in the scenery.

Although Daytona has accommodation to suit every pocket, from the modest motel to the sort of grandiose edifice shown right, many make the annual pilgrimage to Bike Week in their RVs with their bikes in tow. This gives them two kinds of freedom: where and when to ride, and where and when to sleep. RVs and pickup trucks also provide make-shift workshop facilities for any remedial attention that might be required – sand not being known for its beneficial effects on motorcycle components.

Main Street's bars do dynamite business during Bike Week, yet in recent years Daytona Beach's Police Department have reported a decline in drunk driving convictions. Regular visitors all have their favorite watering holes, some of them with tackily nautical themes which are rendered rather incongruous by the lines of wall-to-wall Harleys parked outside. And if you really **have** to interrupt the serious business of chugging beer or chugging down the strip by taking a bite to eat, bars like the Schooner Inn, caught in a mood redolent of Edward Hopper's painting, 'Nighthawks', also feature a conveniently located fast food hatch.

Local traders' enthusiasm for Bike Week is understandable; apart from the annual Spring Break, which attracts not-so-affluent students from all over America, the 70,000–95,000 free-spending motorcyclists who arrive each March are arguably their biggest single source of revenue. After a day at the Volusia County Fairground's giant swap-meet just out of town, Chuck Schmidt's extraordinary Great American Motorcycle Rodeo at the same venue, or even the Speedway itself, most bikers return to Main Street with a powerful thirst and a surprisingly strong urge to purchase souvenirs. Those who let themselves get **really** ripped also have plenty of opportunities to take in a little female action at Daytona's many strip joints and girlie bars, but when they emerge over-excited and bleary eyed, they may face a withering sermon from a motorcycling pastor who preaches forth from his sidecar-mounted pulpit.

Perhaps reflecting the diversity of hogs that doubtless inspired its name, the congregation outside the Iron Horse Saloon (left) could hardly be more varied. The bar itself, out on Highway 1, is a Daytona institution, where bikers can enjoy a brew and shoot a little pool at any time of day, and most of the night.

. . . although this doesn't necessarily mean wall-to-wall rolling drunks. The atmosphere is as affable as you might expect in an environment where everybody shares the same passionate interests: the Iron Horse Saloon is in essence an unofficial club for fans of Milwaukee steel, as the parking lot clearly demonstrates.

Daytona Beach motorcycle cops couldn't really ride anything **other** than Harley–Davidsons, which is maybe why they command more respect than certain other police and sheriff's departments who in recent times have capitulated to less patriotic transport. But in any case, decades of experience in handling the annual influx of two-wheeled visitors has enabled the police to refine their administration of the law to a fairly low-key business.

However, the cops are no slouches when it comes to dealing with any miscreants who flout the law, as in the case of the guy on the right caught riding without a helmet, now mandatory in Florida. Owing to the limited number of police cells, the police truck in a couple of large, black 'mobile jails' during Bike Week, where hapless students arriving early for the Spring Break might end up sharing accommodations with big, hairy-assed bikers!

IMAGES OF STURGIS

LIKE DAYTONA, the annual biker pilgrimage to a tiny, fly-blown township in South Dakota has its origins in motorcycle races. Back in the mid-'thirties the Rapid City Motorcyclists – now known as the Jackpine Gypsies M/cycle Club – received AMA sanction for their 'Black Hills Motor Classic', held at the half-mile oval they themselves refurbished at the Sturgis Fairgrounds. A picnic and a grand parade through town were bolted onto the races which helped to attract substantial numbers of bikers, but the advent of WWII put the event on hold for a while.

When racing resumed at Sturgis after the war, the fringe activities became the main attraction as bike clubs from all over the mid-West made the journey to meet up, make friends, show-off their Harleys (and they **were** predominantly Harleys) and have fun. Inevitably, the increasing concentration of bikerdom on a small rural township led to friction between the local burghers, their overstretched police department and the thousands of riders to whom the word 'Sturgis' was fast becoming a synonym for 'party'. But today upwards of 30,000 bikers arrive at Sturgis each year, comfortable in the knowledge that commercial considerations are now likely to curb the more aggressive instincts of local police.

The recipe for the success of Sturgis remains much the same as it ever was, although racing around the dusty oval track is pretty much a sideshow compared to what happens on Main Street and in the nearby campsites and motels. And because it's August the soul of this particular Bike Week has a discernibly different flavor from the mad March florics down in Florida.

The sense of a long road traveled is perhaps what binds Sturgis aficionados together, enabling them to share a set of values and a sense of spirit that they only experience maybe once a year. Which is why to visit Sturgis is to enjoy a unique motorcycling experience, so unique that you come back for more each August.

The abiding Image of Sturgis, if you will, is the sight of Main Street, an endless vista of wheel-to-wheel V-twins lovingly attended by their proud owners, all of it drenched in bright, mid-summer sunshine and awash with a palpable sense of bonhomie.

Though the Black Hills Motor Classic gave birth to the benign monster that is now Sturgis Bike Week, its relevance is only minor for most folk who ride in every August. Nevertheless the bison, eagle's head and bikers shown in the organising club's logo remind anyone who may notice it of the area's history, both in this and the last century. Custer's Last Stand, as well as those of the American buffalo and eagle, are all South Dakota legends whose strength is still potent.

... But then after over a half a decade of making motorcyclists mighty happy, Bike Week is itself something of a legend. It's also a chance for Sturgis' businessmen to switch into overdrive and make the most of the tired, hungry and thirsty hordes. Check out, for example, the enterprising glass and mirror shop (right), which instantly becomes a filling station for the inner man, offering $3.50 breakfasts and such 'local' delicacies as 'Polish Hot Dogs' and 'Pizza'.

Unlike Daytona with its year-round neon tourism, Sturgis is a somewhat sleepy little backwater which cherishes its down-home values and atmosphere. Which is why when the Rally and Race crowd hit town, the contrasts between normal life and Bike Week are jarring, especially at night when street lighting is largely provided by Milwaukee, rather than the local utilities, as packs of gleaming hogs rumble down Main Street. Naturally enough, Sturgis' official Harley dealer is also very much alight after dark, and does more business in a week than it does most all of the year.

Could this granite-jawed, leather-clad fella on his black Harley Springer (left) be latterday Prince of Darkness? Probably not, but with leather tassels streaming from his handlebars and tastefully studded pannier bags, he cuts a pretty dashing image throbbing through the Sturgis darkness. But, oh dear, aren't those white socks and loafers he's wearing.

Still, at least he's **moving**, a physical state only achieved in fits and starts when traffic on Main Street reaches its peak every evening (above). Not that many visitors complain; they're in Sturgis to hang out and show-off their iron as much as for anything else, and the slow procession down the strip provides an ideal opportunity to do both.

No, it's not a real hog (left), but it's close ... and it typifies Sturgis' easygoing party atmosphere, though I'm not sure if the guy with a skeleton on his pillion (below, left) is making a serious point or otherwise; actually I think it must be otherwise, because they're both exploiting the relaxed local helmet laws.

Ditto the stubble-faced guy on the 'Glide wearing the decidedly bovine headgear (below), who looks like he's trying to make his own comment about South Dakota's buffalo heritage. Easy for him, of course; he can shed his furry coat and pop on his shades when the temperature soars. The roaming herds that once grazed the South Dakota plains weren't so lucky.

Animal life seems to feature strongly in the endless motorised pageant that is Sturgis Bike Week, as this road-hardened gentleman piloting the chopper-ised Panhead sidecar outfit affirms (below, left). And although you may've always believed that a man's best friend was his Harley–Davidson, the dog in the goggles obviously knows better.

There's usually a plentiful supply of an altogether wilder variety of animal on hand at Sturgis, if that's not being too hard on the lady baring much of her rear view (below, right). Still, it's a fair bet she ain't a nun from Pennsylvania visiting her mom and pop, and without such raunchy ladies Sturgis wouldn't be Sturgis ... or even worth coming to for that matter.

Tooling down the highway on a lightly customised, late-model FXR with his feet well forward, wind in the hair, sun beating down on bare forearms, and just enough of a fairing to keep the bugs out of his teeth ... no wonder this guy's got a smile going beneath that bushy moustache (right). South Dakota's usually reliable summer climate, plus the absence of state legislation requiring mandatory wearing of helmets, make the ride to, from and around Sturgis one of the pleasures of anyone's motorcycling year.

Because Sturgis Bike Week takes place in a relatively remote and usually tourist-free region, the majority of riders have to take their accommodation with them. Which is why the roads to Sturgis are filled with Harleys heavily laden with sleeping bags, tents and other stuff essential for a week at one of the campsites available both in the township itself and in the beautiful National Parks nearby. Mount Rushmore's famous presidential sculptures (right) make a dramatic if stoney-faced backdrop en route to Bike Week for a bunch of these motorised back-packers.

Well everyone makes mistakes and, yes, there is the odd smattering of un-American iron to be found at Sturgis. Fortunately Harley–Davidson owners are such a generous-spirited lot that not only do they accept the Japanese presence during Bike Week, they even let 'em ride alongside the real steel (above).

At the end of the day, what Sturgis comes down to for many people is the seductive contrast between some of America's most awesome scenery and America's mightiest motorcycle. Take one big, brawny V-twin – in this case Harley's FXSTC Softail Custom (left) – pitch it in among the soaring mountains and aromatic pines of Dakota's Black Hills, and you've got an evocative picture of why American motorcycling has such a strong hold on those who are lucky enough to indulge in it. As for those who don't, well, they're plainly missing out ... And they've plainly never been to Sturgis during Bike Week.

RAT BIKES

ALTHOUGH WE'VE SEEN THAT Harley–Davidson ownership cuts across a wide range of cultural, social and income barriers, pride in the appearance of one's machinery is one thing that hog owners do tend to have in common. But there are notable exceptions, and those are the folk who run Rat Bikes.

No one really knows the origin of the rat bike, but my guess is that, faced with the prospect of restoring a badly maintained motorcycle to its former glory, a terminally lazy biker makes the mental decision to 'screw it' and goes off in precisely the opposite direction. And the route he takes can be as varied and even imaginative as that taken by the customiser, for a grungey old rat bike is as much a reflection of its owner's tastes as is the gleaming, painstakingly decorated or modified Harley.

Rat bikes usually begin their identity change as ill-maintained hogs just about kept going by non-standard parts and irregular service intervals. Add to that a rich patina of corrosion, paintwork touched up by a brush rather than a spray-gun, and a few ugly, if faintly practical accessories such as busted saddle-bags and cracked, yellowed windscreens, and you've got yourself the basis for a rat bike.

Over a period of time you can decorate your rat bike with ever more personal expressions of affection; tacky old jewelry, metal ashtrays, lamps that look more at home on a kitchen wall than on a motorcycle, and button badges, bumper stickers and decals espousing some heartfelt cause. In this way, you not only find yourself with a Harley–Davidson that's as distinctive as anything either the factory or the customiser could ever dream up, but also a mobile conversation piece. Be warned, however, if you're thinking of traveling down the rat bike road, because hanging a load of what is, literally, rubbish on your bike and hiding the improprieties of your maintenance program beneath a heavy film of filth is also just as likely to attract the attentions of the police department. But then isn't owning a Harley–Davidson all about freedom at any price?

Rat bike decor is as good a measure
of an owner's quirks and passage
through life as any psychiatrist could
muster. And there can't be much
wrong with a man who's been to
the Berlin Wall and received so many
baubles from affectionate
lady friends.

Not sure if the guy reclining along the ancient Panhead (left) is trying to hitch a lift away from his mobile eyesore, or expressing a laid-back pride in its dishevelment and inviting your approval. Check out the shotgun, police pursuit lamp and teddybear, but don't ask what it all **means**.

It may seem highly unlikely that the rat bike shown below and right (and on the previous spread), actually managed to make it from Kentucky to Daytona Bike Week, but in fact Smitty, its owner, takes it to motorcycling events all over the country. One is tempted to conclude that he takes all his worldly goods along with him, in which case the world Smitty lives in is, well, pretty damn interesting.

Referring in this case to scrap metal rather than illegal substances, the 'Junky Jim' who owns this fine example of rolling detritus is in fact a wealthy dealer in used Harley–Davidson parts. The mere fact that the crusty old 45cu. in. side-valve is actually able to transport its owner and all that rubbish is some kind of testimony to the quality of his wares. But then maybe the lariat hanging over the gas tank is a prudent precaution in case he needs a tow.

Shovelheads – possibly because they're less loved but more commonplace than other Harleys – frequently provide the basis for (or become the butt of) the rat bike builders' ministrations. Here's a fine example of the breed, shown before and after Daytona Bike Week (above left and right), which demonstrates how quickly a little scavenging and ingenuity can be put to good effect!

FOXY LADIES

'OLD LADIES', 'CHICKS', 'BIKE BABES' . . . whatever and however dismissively they're referred to, the women who hang out with serious motorcyclists have a character that's inevitably as special as the Harley's they straddle. Invariably blonde but rarely dumb, the girls who take up the biker lifestyle need to be tough as well as tender, because not only do they sometimes have to play second fiddle to a greater love in the life of their menfolk, namely a big, hot Harley, but they're also the object of a loyalty that rivals a man's love for his hog, a loyalty that needs to be rewarded. Not that these foxy ladies have to be entirely subservient to attract and keep their biker boy lovers, but knowing when to get on with their own female business and when to get involved with that of their man's . . . well, that's a highly prized art.

And so is the look that identifies, but certainly not unifies these women. Foxy fashions change at a rather more leisurely pace than the constant shifts and extremes of **haute couture**. Black leather and faded denim certainly, but cleaner, tighter, more tastefully studded and tassled than the stuff worn by the male of the species and, in the case of denim, often judiciously frayed or teasingly ripped. In fact, if one word were to sum up the foxy approach to clothing, 'tantalising' would probably be it.

A glance around any biker rally or semi-organised meet is proof-positive of this as the ladies strut around apparently vying with each other for the title of least clad or most provocatively clad little vixen. And when the weather's good and warm, then the wraps really come off and ingenious experiments in minimalist use of Lycra and leather reveal themselves, and a lot more besides. The acreage of firmly tanned female flesh is, however, a little at odds with a uniquely hybrid sado-masochistic image that's the flip-side of the foxy phenomenon and could best be described as Morticia-out-of-Valkyrie Goddess. But if these symbolic evocations are innocently confusing or deliberately and coquettishly misleading, then so be it – that's part of the biker girl's very special allure.

'Stand by your man' takes on a newer, sassier meaning when you're wearing just a few fringes and demonstrating a certain cheeky chutzpah; surely any red-blooded biker would relish the chance to have the lady on the right standing beside him?

Strolling down the Strip with a lady like the one above is a sure way to attract a little peer group envy, and a photographer's attention. And if you're secure in the knowledge that you're the one who'll be taking her home, then it should also be a source of no little pride!

Meanwhile, elsewhere on the street another a pair of leather chaps frames another cheeky face and attracts the inevitable gaggle of admirers. The fact that they're not all lascivious males underlines the fact that pillion-packing ladies are as comfortable with each other as they are with their men.

Although motorcycling never was a strictly male preserve, maybe the foxiest of the foxes are the ones who take on the guys at their own game and ride their own bikes. In the case of the lady above it's a late model Springer Softail; so what if it's pink?

And then there's the sporting ladies . . . Always game for a laugh, or simply displaying their particular talents and physical blessings with nary a trace of embarrassment, quite a few foxy ladies are more than willing to put on a show for the boys; or is it for the other girls? Whether it's a matter of finely judged skill, like taking a bite out of a dangling weenie from the back seat of a Harley like the lady on the left . . . .

. . . or displaying rather more raunch, and quite a lot more besides, and battling it out in an arena full of mud (above), these are foxy ladies who like to party according to a different set of rules. Or maybe no rules at all. That's almost certainly another reason why the guys love 'em.

And not all the babes who hang out with the Harley boys are blonde, long-maned temptresses . . . Some of 'em are brown, short-haired temptresses. But, any man would be transfixed by that tattoo whoever was wearing it; the fact that the lady is smart and gorgeous as well is a massive bonus.

Some of the girls love bikes as much as their men, and don't mind exercising a little elbow grease in the cause of presenting their mutual pride and joy to its best effect. Or maybe the lady doing the shining (above) actually owns that Harley herself.

S & M in the sunshine might seem rather contrary, but then the world of bike culture is full of contradictions and the lady in the Lycra, leather and chains seems more than happy with the results . . . and the attention she's getting from the camera.

As Harleys aren't exactly the lightest or easiest of motorcycles to heave around, especially at low speeds, the woman on the FXRS (right) is perhaps not so much a foxy lady, more a serious woman biker. Clearly she knows how to handle a hog, and looks like she could deal with anything else that happens her way as well. Ironically enough, those are attributes many males of the species find pretty damn attractive in a woman, so it looks like she's also got the best of both worlds.

TATTOOES AND BODY PIERCING

IT'S A VANITY THING, it's a tribal thing, it's a sado-masochistic thing, it's an historic rite of passage, it's a liberation of the self ... all these and many more are reasons routinely given for the practises of tattooing and, to a lesser extent, body piercing. And they're probably all correct, for this particular style of self-adornment has long been something its acolytes have found themselves having to explain to those who find such things repugnant, explanations which invariably differ from soul to soul.

What is undeniably true is the disproportionate popularity of these forms of 'body art' among the world's biking population, a popularity which perhaps begs a whole 'nother set of questions. But then again, does it really matter why folks do things that hurt no one other than themselves ... and then only a little, and only temporarily?

Fact is, die-hard motorcyclists are major consumers of the tattooist's art, which is self-evident when the sun comes out and the T-shirts come off. Indeed, according to one long-established professional tattooist, bikers have taken over from seamen as the biggest single market for his craft which, he reckoned, had much to do with the freewheeling lifestyles of both groups. However psychologically diverse or complex the motivation to get a tattoo, bikers tend to fall into two camps when it comes to going under the needle; those who are giving their vanity a little treat, and those who relentlessly pursue self-decoration until most of their available surface area is a dense, colorful tapestry.

In the first category, a biker – or his girl – may celebrate a commitment to a new lover, the birth of a child or even a new Harley with an appropriate tattoo. This may lead to a habit of 'treat-tattooing' until a pair of intertwined bluebirds gradually develops into a frieze and suddenly you're a walking work of art! Those truly addicted to tattoos are inevitably keener to work premeditated themes and images into their adornments, but in either case, a tattoo is forever ... rather like a Harley–Davidson.

The days of self-inflicted body art are long gone, so whether you're only the occasional recipient of a tattoo (like the lady shown here), or a slave to the art (like her ol' man), the intricacy and imagination inherent in the work of the tattooist is something both undeniably share.

Here indeed are wonderful examples of the tattooist's art and the finesse with which color and graphic design can be wrought across the canvas of the human body. The entire tattoo shown here was clearly conceived all-of-a-piece, although it would have been essential for its application to be carried out in stages – the patience of the tattooist and the skin of the subject would otherwise have suffered, especially the latter! Familiar themes such as tigers, bondage, eagles and reptiles are cleverly, even wickedly combined, whereas less obvious influences, such as underground cartoonist S. Clay Wilson and monochrome portraiture, distinguish the tattoo 'cardigan' adorning the guy's torso.

Suntan and freckles somehow add dignity to a tattoo (or two!) as shown upper left, although it's hard to deny that a paler skin can prove an equally entrancing backdrop to this ultimate in body illustration (below). The practitioners of this very twentieth-century art often travel the bike rally and show circuit, setting up shop in motel rooms or booths where potential clients can inspect samples of his craft before deciding to take the plunge. In fact the electronic tattoo 'gun' only grazes the surface of the skin and the sensation is one of irritation, rather than pain.

Outright piercing of the flesh is something else again, and in some senses a heavier, although clearly less permanent commitment. Ears and nipples are the more visible body parts that tend to receive the 'frozen needle' that permits the attachment of a ring (above, left) or, more intriguingly, bells and a chain (above, right). But for many of those bikers that are **really** into it, piercing often takes place in less obvious, more private areas. Ouch!

HARLEY RACING

THE NAME HARLEY–DAVIDSON means many things to many people, but the term 'racing motorcycles' is not usually among them, unless you're a student of Harley history, or one of that band of specialists committed to wringing levels of performance out of the big V-twin that God and Milwaukee surely never meant it to deliver. But even that's not quite true, for during the company's first two decades competition success played a vital part in their growth, and the 'Wrecking Crew' – as the factory race team was nicknamed – had an unassailable grip on almost all forms of motorcycle sport. Then it was a 61cu. in. (999cc) 8-valve engine in a rigid frame that formed the backbone of Harley's racing effort, but by the mid-'twenties this had been superseded by the Model JDH 'two-cam', a 74cu. in. machine that was the first bike to broach the magical 100mph, at Altoona Speedway, Pennsylvania, in 1925. Since then Harley's involvement in bike sports has waxed and waned much according to their commercial fortunes, with such bikes as the XR750 dominating dirt-track for almost two decades, and the Italian sourced Aermacchi/Harley–Davidsons having mixed fortunes during the early 'seventies in both on- and off-road racing. In the early 'eighties the new 'Battle of the Twins' (BoTT) road-races tempted Harley to attack the European marques that ruled the roost, and in 1983 factory flat-tracker Jay Springsteen mesmerised one and all by virtually walking the race on the XR1000. Despite walloping the opposition so convincingly, the company has since proved erratic in its commitment to competition, for while machines powered by Harley engines have enjoyed varying degrees of success in BoTT, flat-track, drag-racing and hill-climb, only when they could see a direct correlation between what they raced and what they could sell would they pitch in serious money and effort. But with the current popularity of the 'Sportster 883 Series' races on both sides of the Atlantic, perhaps the factory will be able to justify a greater involvement in the sporting life.

Ironically, the acknowledged master of America's 'Sportster 883 Series' is in fact a Briton. Little known in England, California-based Nigel Gale dominates this popular production class in the US with a tenacious, fluid style, as shown while leading Daytona's 1990 event (right).

Racing Sportsters isn't as easy as Nigel Gale makes it look (see pp. 116–17), for while the current Evo-engined models have significantly more urge and better chassis than earlier incarnations of Harley's 'sporty lightweight', they remain taller, under-braked and down on power compared to most contemporary bikes in their class. Fortunately the rules do allow some substitutions, such as 'Screamin' Eagle' carbs, Kerker exhaust systems and uprated suspension, brakes and tires, but for a bike originally cast in the mould of a foot-out, sideways-sliding dirt-tracker, it still takes a lot of skill – and money – to keep it running hard'n'fast on road circuits.

With just a few narrow inches of rubber (and the rider's knee) kissing the tarmac, this racing Sportster (above) is cornering pretty much on the limit for a big V-twin designed and manufactured exclusively for street use. But Harley guys, they just love a challenge . . .

. . . Some more than others, however! The riders in this 'Sportster 883 Series' race (below) demonstrate varying degrees of body-lean as they hustle round a tight corner of Daytona's infield: No. 194 looks as if he's about to stick his leg out, dirt-track style!

The Buell Motorcycle Co. first unveiled its radically framed, Harley-engined specials in 1989. Since then Roger Buell's brave little outfit has managed to field a racing team (right) and show the Milwaukee factory what the future could well look like for state-of-the art V-twins.

Although factory-supported Harleys have taken their share of out and out speed records over the years (most notably Dan Kinsey who hit 276.5mph on his single-engined 'Tenacious' in 1985), these days the rather conservative V-twin engine is only really competitive in drag races arranged specifically to accommodate it. Such is the dramatic appeal of an intrepid rider dumping the clutch on a roaring, high-tuned Harley that these events are nonetheless very popular with Harley–Davidson cognoscenti. The guy on the right was roasting his particular rear tire at Sturgis Bike Week in '91.

Motorcycle racing is even more of an exclusively male domain than recreational riding, the theory presumably being that so-called feminine frailty mitigates against the physical demands of wrestling with a highly tuned machine that's running 'on the limits'. But although drag racing involves massive G-forces and requires an ability to hold what might otherwise be a bucking bronco in a straight line, it's a sport increasingly engaged in by women (left). And as well as a touch of glamor, they can also bring faster reactions to a form of racing where split second reactions are of the ultimate importance.

Draggin' Harley–Davidsons is a spectacular affair, with 'wheelie bars' bolted onto the rear frame to stop front wheels pawing too far into the air (as the guy on the Shovelhead, right, is trying to cope with), and the acrid smell of burning rubber from the rear tire mingling with the heady aroma of exotic fuels. Quite apart from all that, there's the noise!

ON THE ROAD AGAIN

EVENTUALLY, OF COURSE, the holiday reaches the end of its allotted time, the rally hits the last date in its diary, or work darkly beckons after that long weekend. In other words, time's up ... and you've got to clamber aboard your bike and hit the road back to wherever you came from.

Which isn't such a bad thing if you've got the right motorcycle, the right weather and the right road ahead, and since we're talking Harley–Davidson here, there's no doubt that in most vital respects the return trip has as much to offer as any other journey. The adrenalin flows whenever you hit the button and those two big cylinders rumble into life, perhaps with a short cough and a splutter, and you purposefully snick the lever into first gear, release the clutch and move out onto the beckoning tarmac. A palpable shiver of excitement will soon remind you why it is you're on a bike, more specifically on a Harley, and the fact that you're homeward bound is but a minor irritant.

And t'was ever thus: as we've seen elsewhere in this book, Harleys have always appealed to the touring rider and the adventurer in us all, but Milwaukee's current generation of smooth riding, oil-tight, Evo-engined models makes it much easier to take the big ride. Fifteen years ago the Japanese thought they had it all over the last remaining American motorcycle company with their touring machines. But Honda's Gold Wing, Yamaha's Voyager and the rest hadn't allowed for a company that was moving ahead at its own pace, and the power of brand loyalty. So riders who were once perhaps tempted by, or indeed even defected to, the heavyweight oriental tourers, suddenly found that they could have the best of both worlds: motorcycles that were reliable and were clearly born in the USA, and yet offered them all the comforts and gee-gaws that the Japanese so cunningly bolted on to what were, in most other respects, essentially soulless machines. And that's why if you're on the road again, a Harley is still the only way to go.

It is, after all, a damn fine feeling, and the rider on the right exactly evokes that emotion as he chases across the horizon in the late afternoon. It's as if you can experience an infectious sense of urgency as he guns his Springer Softail toward who-knows-where.

Whether it's dawdling through a sunny afternoon (left), or thrumming steadily onward to the distant horizon in Big Sky country (above), the road goes on forever if you're on a Harley–Davidson and among friends. And there's a rhythm to the road that not only orchestrates the ride, but acts like a drug, gnawing away in the back of the subconscious when you're away from your wheels, beckoning you back to where you belong ...

... or where you're going, because you could be forgiven for thinking that this final episode in our modest literary journey is just about going home, which of course it's not. Being 'On The Road Again' is as much about going forward as it is about going back. But then again, there's something about returning tired, safe but happy from a long trip that's even more satisfying than the excitement of anticipation that preceded it.

Stops along the way provide an opportunity to compare experiences, maybe brag a little about speeds and sights along the way, pretty much the usual stuff of 'road talk' that the guys on the left have been doing now that they've gassed up at this funky old filling station and getting ready for another, maybe coupla hundred mile chug. Interestingly, although two of the bikes here are modern, Evo-engined Harleys, the Shovel on the extreme right and the 'Glide furthest from the camera are from an era when long distance touring was rather more of an ordeal and a good deal tougher.

ON THE ROAD AGAIN

In the summer months, particularly in the north eastern and western states where harsher winters relegate motorcycling to strictly mundane, largely metropolitan travel, it's little wonder that road-hungry Harley–Davidson owners keep clothing to a minimum and mileage to a maximum when the sun finally shines on them (see left). Sure, it doesn't exactly minimise the potential damage to life and limb, but if you want to stay utterly safe, what you do is buy a car. And as any die-hard motorcyclist knows, being insulated from your environment in a motorised tin can means missing out on the sounds and smells of the countryside, or in the case of the guys of the right, that glorious cacophony as a tunnel cut through solid rock echoes and magnifies the mighty rumble and roar of Milwaukee steel (right).

To other riders, the art of 'living dangerously' means running hard and fast on a rigid-framed chopper with extended springer forks and the absolute minimum in the braking department (right). Mind you, it doesn't seem as if the owner of this minimalist Shovelhead is taking a particularly long journey unless, that is, he's got a friend trucking his luggage along behind him ... one who's maybe also a qualified doctor!

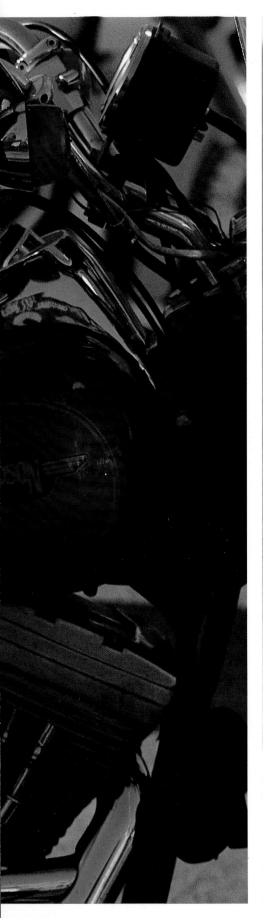

On the slightly morbid subject of the fragile nature of flesh and blood, it looks like one of the many bits of ephemera the guy on the left has collected along the road is a hospital identification tag ... check out his left forearm. Now is that tough, or what?!

And being an Angel, the guy above is **undoubtedly** tough, although what the message on the registration plate means is anybody's guess. Surely the only hogs that don't sweat are Harley–Davidsons ... except the really old ones, and the only thing they oozed was a bit of oil!

On the road again for this couple (above) means more swinging through bright sunshine on a late FXR-series model, but judging by the smile on the pillion rider's face and the total absence of gloves, this looks like a short jaunt rather than a long run. In contrast, the trio of very different Harleys on the right look like they're transporting their owners on a major trek and they're running a little behind schedule; hell, the guy in the middle doesn't even have time to stop for a smoke!

Man in a hurry on this FXLR Low Rider bears all the signs of a serious traveler: somewhere underneath all that luggage is the sissy-bar that makes it all possible. Probably the most popular range currently produced by Harley, the FXR line has a model for just about every road-burning need, from the ultra-comfortable, semi-faired FXRT Sport Glide to the FXRS-SP Low Rider Sport Edition which features tunable front forks and longer-travel suspension at both ends. What they have in common is the meaty, 80cu. in. Evolution engine and entirely adequate heft for the long haul.

At the end of the day it doesn't really matter which Harley–Davidson you're riding, as long as it **is** one. And whether you're reflecting on your latest journey like the above road-hardened lone traveler appears to be doing ...

... or flashing through the night with your darling nestling close-up behind you (below), there's something about arriving as darkness follows you down the road that adds poignancy, even a sense of drama to the whole touring experience.

But when there's a whole bunch of you sharing that experience, the atmosphere becomes even more charged, the sense of satisfaction more meaningful. If that sounds a little pompous, buy yourself a Harley and try it!